TIME
FOR KIDS
BOOK OF WHY

AWESOME ANIMAL KINGDOM

TIME FOR KIDS

Managing Editor: Nellie Gonzalez Cutler
Editor: Brenda Iasevoli
Creative Director: Jennifer Kraemer-Smith

Time Home Entertainment

Publisher: Jim Childs
Vice President, Brand &
Digital Strategy: Steven Sandonato
Executive Director, Marketing Services: Carol Pittard
Executive Director, Retail & Special Sales: Tom Mifsud
Executive Publishing Director: Joy Bomba
Director, Bookazine Development
& Marketing: Laura Adam
Vice President, Finance Director: Vandana Patel
Publishing Director: Megan Pearlman
Assistant General Counsel: Simone Procas
Assistant Director, Special Sales: Ilene Schreider
Brand Manager: Jonathan White
Associate Prepress Manager: Alex Voznesenskiy
Associate Production Manager: Kimberly Marshall
Associate Project Manager: Stephanie Braga

Editorial Director: Stephen Koepp
Senior Editor: Roe D'Angelo
Copy Chief: Rina Bander
Design Manager: Anne-Michelle Gallero
Editorial Operations: Gina Scauzillo

Special thanks: Katherine Barnet, Brad Beatson, Jeremy Biloon, Susan Chodakiewicz, Rose Cirrincione, Assu Etsubneh, Mariana Evans, Christine Font, Susan Hettleman, Hillary Hirsch, David Kahn, Amy Mangus, Nina Mistry, Dave Rozzelle, Ricardo Santiago, Adriana Tierno

Contents of this book previously appeared in Time For Kids Big Book of WHY.

For information on TIME FOR KIDS magazine for the classroom or home, go to TIMEFORKIDS.COM or call 1-800-777-8600.
For subscriptions to SI KIDS, go to SIKIDS.COM or call 1-800-889-6007.

Published by TIME FOR KIDS Books,
An imprint of Time Home Entertainment Inc.
135 West 50th Street
New York, NY 10020

ISBN 10: 1-60320-983-2
ISBN 13: 978-1-60320-983-0

TIME FOR KIDS is a trademark of Time Inc.

We welcome your comments and suggestions about TIME FOR KIDS Books. Please write to us at:
TIME FOR KIDS Books, Attention: Book Editors, P.O. Box 11016, Des Moines, IA 50336-1016
If you would like to order any of our hardcover Collector's Edition books, please call us at 1-800-327-6388 (Monday through Friday, 7 a.m. to 8 p.m., or Saturday, 7 a.m. to 6 p.m., Central Time).

1 QGT 14

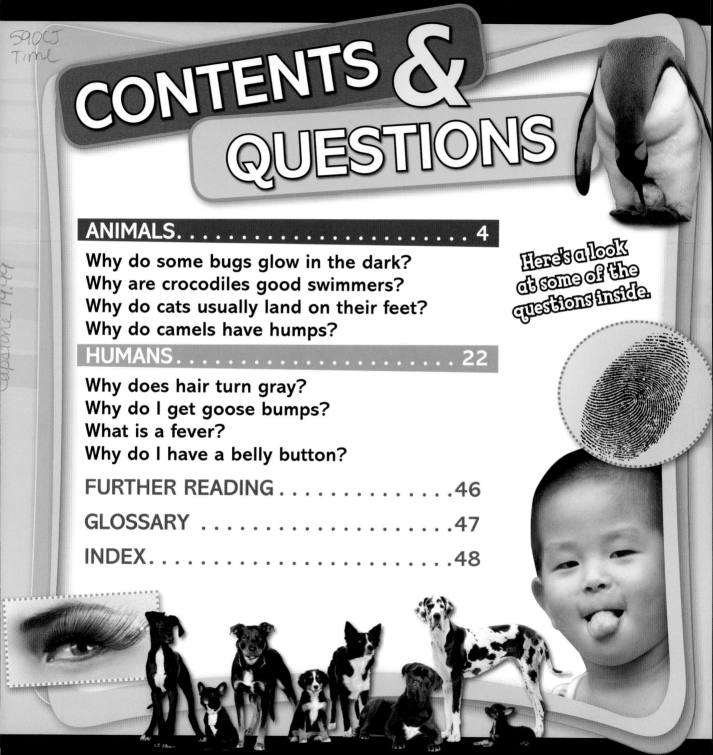

590CJ
Time

CapStove 19.99

CONTENTS & QUESTIONS

Here's a look at some of the questions inside.

Why are dogs' noses wet?

While the noses of many dogs are wet, plenty of dogs have dry ones. What keeps a dog's snout moist? No one knows for sure. One theory is that the wetness comes from **mucus** produced inside Fido's nose. Another **hypothesis** suggests that because dogs lick their noses all the time, saliva keeps their noses moist. Despite popular belief, a warm nose does not mean a dog is sick.

Why do dogs turn around before lying down?

Around and around and around again! Dogs will often turn in a circle on the bed or carpet two or three times before curling up and going to sleep. Are they checking for bed bugs or snakes? Not necessarily. Many times dogs are just flattening out their beds to get comfortable. This behavior is a genetic trait left over from when the dog's ancestors used to dig their own shelters. After digging, the dogs would feel comfortable in their "dens" and plop down for some much needed shut-eye.

WHY DO WOLVES AND DOGS OFTEN LOOK ALIKE?

Scientists say that dogs evolved from wolves about 15,000 years ago. After comparing dog and wolf **DNA**, scientists concluded that every dog—from Chihuahuas to Great Danes—is descended from a group of approximately five female Asian wolves. They were the mothers of all modern dogs.

Why do monkeys and apes prefer bananas over other food?

Monkeys and apes don't monkey around when they eat bananas. They really do enjoy the treat. Although monkeys and apes like eating other fruit, bananas seem to be tops on the menu. Bananas have a sweet smell and, well, taste great. Monkeys and apes like to use their thumbs to pull back the peel, too. It's like playing.

What makes apes and monkeys different?

Although apes and monkeys are both **primates**, a special kind of **mammal**, they are also different from one another.

An adult gorilla can weigh up to 452 pounds (205 kg).

MONKEYS
Live in Africa, Asia, Central and South America
Tails allow them to live near the tops of trees
Smaller in size, usually weighing no more than 30 pounds

APES
Live mostly in Africa
Do not have tails; live mostly on the ground
Much bigger than monkeys; have broad backs
Can learn sign language and use tools, such as sticks and rocks

WHY ARE APES SO MUCH LIKE HUMANS?

We might look a little different from a gorilla or any of the other great apes, but humans and apes have many things in common. We share about 99 percent of our genes with apes, and according to some scientists, apes—chiefly chimpanzees—form cultures just like humans. A culture is a learned way of living passed down from one generation to the next. Most researchers agree that humans and chimps diverged from a common ancestor about 5 million to 7 million years ago.

Why do vampire bats drink blood?

There are many different types of bats, but there's only one type that drinks blood—the vampire bat. They are the only mammals that feed entirely on blood. A special **enzyme** in the saliva of a vampire bat keeps the blood of animals from clotting, making the blood easier to drink. Scientists say the first vampire bats that emerged were related to bats that gorged themselves on the parasites of prehistoric beasts. Vampire bats slowly evolved into drinking the blood of animals.

WHY DO BATS USE ECHOLOCATION?

Bats, which have poor eyesight, use echolocation to keep from slamming into objects and to detect their favorite meal—bugs. Bats emit a high frequency sound that humans cannot hear and then wait for the sound to echo off of any nearby objects. Based on how long the echo takes to reach it, bats can determine the distance, location, movement, and size of the object. Submarines use sonar in much the same way.

Why do vampire bats rarely attack humans?

Vampire bats would rather feast on sleeping animals than humans. Vampire bats live in the tropics of Central and South America. One hundred vampire bats can drink the blood of 25 cows in one year. Vampire bats do not remove enough blood to kill an animal, but the bites can cause an infection.

How many different kinds of fish are there?

There are more than 24,000 known species of fish living in the world's oceans, lakes, streams, ponds, and rivers. Fish were the first **vertebrates** to appear on Earth. Each species evolved over millions of years, adapting to its specific environment.

WHY DO SOME FISH LIVE ONLY IN FRESHWATER AND OTHERS ONLY IN SALTWATER?

Evolution is the reason why some fish can live only in freshwater, while other fish live only in salty seawater. However, some fish live in both types of water. Some species began as saltwater fish, but later developed ways to live in freshwater.

This freshwater fish wouldn't live long in saltwater

How are crocodiles and alligators different?

Although they look as if they are brother and sister, crocodiles and alligators are distant cousins.

ALLIGATORS
Live in the United States and China
Have wide, U-shaped snouts
Prefer to live in freshwater habitats

CROCODILES
Live in Mexico, Central America, South America, Africa, Southeast Asia and Australia
Have V-shaped snouts
Prefer to live in saltwater habitats

WHY ARE CROCODILES GOOD SWIMMERS?

The tail of a crocodile is huge and strong. In the water, crocodiles use their tails for power. Crocodiles swim by pressing their legs flat against their bodies, creating fish-like figures. Using one webbed foot as a rudder, they propel themselves forward by moving their strong tails back and forth. Crocodiles can swim more than 6 miles (9.7 km) per hour.

Female crocodiles can lay 25 to 80 eggs!

Alligators have been around for 150 million years.

Why do some **bugs**
glow in the dark?

Who doesn't love glow-in-the-dark Halloween costumes, stickers, or glow sticks? Many bugs glow in the dark, too. They make their own light. These bugs are **bioluminescent** (BY-oh-lew-muh-NESS-ent). Chemicals in their bodies combine to make them shine. Although bioluminescent animals light up, they don't give off heat as a lightbulb does. Fireflies are the most common glow-in-the-dark insects. They light up to communicate with each other as they look for a mate.

WHY IS BIOLUMINESCENCE IMPORTANT?

Scientists study bioluminescence in animals for a number of reasons, including trying to find ways to cure cancer and other diseases in humans. For example, eye doctors use what scientists have learned about bioluminescence to detect, without using surgery, if an eye tumor is cancerous.

WHY DO SOME FISH GIVE OFF THEIR OWN LIGHT?

Deep in the ocean, some bioluminescent fish turn on the lights to attract their next meal. Oth animals use light to blind predators that try to stalk and eat them. Some species create light to blend in with their surroundings. Scientists really don't know why some animals give off their own light. Some worms spit out glowing ooze, although no one can figure out why. It's a mystery why tiny plankton glow when disturbed by storms, waves, or passing boats.

Why do cats always land on their feet?

Cats are the acrobats of all household pets. If a cat falls from a short distance, it will almost always land on its feet. Because it lacks a collarbone, a cat can easily rotate and bend its body more than other animals. The backbones of cats are also more flexible than other animals'. This allows them to turn and land on their feet.

Unlike dogs, cats have no problem landing on their paws.

Why do **cats meow?**

Cats can't talk, but they can certainly meow. And if they're *purrrrfectly* clear, humans know what they mean. One researcher says that cats have learned to meow in ways that call out to humans. Sometimes cats meow for attention. Such meows are very short and quiet (as in *ME-ow*). Sometimes a cat's meow is more urgent (as in me-*OWWW*). Cats also communicate with one another. They'll hiss when they are angry or feel threatened. They'll howl when they are hurt. Some big cats, like lions, don't meow at all. They roar!

WHY DO CATS COUGH UP HAIR?

Cough! Cough! Hack! Cats groom themselves by licking their fur. Naturally, they end up swallowing some hair in the process. When too much hair collects in a cat's stomach, the stomach lining becomes irritated and—*hack!*—the cat throws up a hairball.

Why can't penguins fly?

Penguins are odd—they have wings but can't fly like ordinary birds. Penguins belong to a group of birds call **sphenisciformes** (sfen-is-kuh-FORM-eez). Sphenisciformes would rather swim than fly. Penguins do not have hollow bones like flying birds. Instead, their bones are weighty, which makes it easier for them to dive into the water and swim. And penguins do love swimming. Adélie penguins can swim hundreds of miles at a steady 4.97 miles (8 km) per hour. Penguins use their wings to move through the water, just as any other bird uses its wings to move through the air.

HOW DOES A PENGUIN STAY WARM IN ANTARCTICA?

Penguins have a large amount of fat below their skin. The fat acts like insulation, keeping the torpedo-shaped critter warm even in the harsh climate of Antarctica. The birds have a special **circulatory system** in their feet. This keeps their bodies warm and their feet slightly cooler, reducing the amount of heat loss in the winter. Penguins also huddle with other penguins to keep toasty.

WHY DO MALE PENGUINS TAKE CARE OF THE PENGUIN EGGS?

During the cold months of Antarctica's winter, male emperor penguins huddle by the hundreds in the snow and ice. The females lay the eggs, and then the males keep the eggs warm on the tops of their feet for about 65 days. A layer of skin on the male's stomach hangs down over the egg to keep it warm. Where are the females during this period? After laying the eggs, the females go off to feed. When they return, they are fat and warm. After the eggs hatch, it's the male's turn to feast.

11

Why do fire ants sting?

Ouch! That burns! All ant bites and stings hurt, but the sting of a fire ant can be particularly painful. Fire ants are very aggressive and will swarm over anything and anyone that disturbs their nests, including wild animals, pets, and people. Fire ants have big jaws that can grab on to things and a bee-like stinger that pumps poison into their **prey** or an attacker. When their nests come under attack, or when the ants feel threatened, they will swarm. They give off special chemicals called **pheromones** (FEH-re-moans), which cause the ants to be overly aggressive. A red ant can sting many times. Its poison will cause a temporary burning feeling. When a group of red ants attack, their many stings can be deadly. The ants would have to sting an animal thousands of times for that to happen, however.

Red ants can carry up to 20 times their body weight!

Do ants have skeletons?

Although they don't have a bag of bones in their closets, ants do have skeletons—exoskeletons. Most animals—including you—have bones under the skin. But the skeleton of an ant is on the outside of its body. Exoskeletons are hard and protect the insect's soft insides.

WHY DO SOME ANTS HAVE WINGS?

Not all ants have wings, but some do. When you see an ant with wings, what you are seeing is an ant that is old enough to reproduce. Ants with wings are also known as *swarmers*. Their job is to fly to distant places and set up other ant colonies.

Why do spiders **spin webs?**

Spider-Man spins his web to swing from building to building and to catch villains. Real spiders spin webs for the same reasons—sort of. Spiders release a sticky type of silk from their **abdomens** when they spin a web. Spiders use webs to climb from place to place. Spiders also spin webs to trap their next meal and to make egg sacs to hold their eggs.

DO FEMALE BLACK WIDOW SPIDERS KILL THEIR MATES?

Most people believe the female black widow spider kills and then eats her mate after mating. This is not always the case. Males often escape the clutches of the female once they finish mating. However, on occasion, the female will eat the male.

What's the difference between an arachnid and an insect?

Many people call spiders insects, but that's not true. Spiders are arachnids and here is how they differ from insects:

Scorpions are also a type of arachnid.

ARACHNIDS	INSECTS
Have 8 legs and 8 eyes;	Have 6 legs and 2 compound eyes;
Do not have antennae or wings.	Have antennae and wings.

Why do some animals change color?

Many animals have developed ways to keep from getting eaten. One way is to change color. This type of **camouflage** helps animals hide from predators. Many animals produce chemicals inside their bodies that change their natural **pigments**. Many animals can change color anytime they want. A flounder for example, can change its color to match the mud, sand, or gravel on the ocean floor.

Flounders have a knack for blending in to their surroundings.

Why do some animals protect other animals?

Some animals depend on one another to survive. This is called a **symbiotic** relationship. For example, the tiny clownfish hangs out with the poisonous sea anemone. The clownfish attracts food that the anemone likes to eat in return for the anemone's protection. The anemone's sting, however, does not harm the clownfish.

HOW DO STRIPES PROTECT A ZEBRA?

You might think that on the savanna of Africa, the black-and-white zebra stands out from the crowd, making it a tempting target for a passing lion. However, the zebra's stripes actually help the animal hide in plain sight. From a distance, a herd of zebras looks like a wavy mass of black and white lines, confusing a hungry lion. The lion can't pick out a single animal to attack, so the big cat retreats, leaving the zebras alone.

Flying squirrels don't really fly. They glide!

WHY DO SQUIRRELS EAT BIRDSEED?

Squirrels will often pounce on a birdfeeder because it is crammed with tasty nuts and seeds. Squirrels are primarily herbivores. They eat plant material such as nuts, fruits, mushrooms, pine cones, leaves, twigs, bark, and, yes, birdseed.

Why do squirrels have such **bushy tails?**

When a squirrel is in a tree it uses its big tail for balance. This helps the furry critter move quickly from branch to branch without falling over. Squirrels also use their tails like parachutes in case they fall out of a tree. A squirrel's tail keeps the animal warm in the winter and allows the creature to communicate with other squirrels. A squirrel will threaten another squirrel by flinging its tail over its back and flicking it.

DO SQUIRRELS REALLY REMEMBER WHERE THEY HIDE THEIR FOOD?

Let's put this myth to rest once and for all. Squirrels don't always remember where they hide their acorns and chestnuts. Scientists used to believe that squirrels, specifically gray squirrels, remembered where they dug their holes to store their nuts and also smelled the food they buried. However, studies have shown that most squirrels never recover their buried nuts. In fact, other squirrels find the nuts and keep them. Most acorns and nuts remain buried and grow into young trees called saplings.

Why are some insects
attracted to light?

Have you ever sat out on a front porch at night and turned on a light? What happens? Within moments, insects by the dozen start buzzing around the glowing bulb. There are a number of theories as to why bugs are attracted to light. Most scientists suspect that when an insect flies at night, it uses a light source, such as the moon, to keep on a straight path. If there is a closer source of light, such as a candle or light bulb, the insect gets confused, causing it to fly to the nearest light.

Why do some insects sting?

Some insects, such as bees, wasps, and ants, carry a loaded weapon with them at all times—a stinger full of poison. Bugs that sting are generally defending themselves or their nests. In most cases, a bee sting will only hurt for a while, unless a person is allergic to bee stings.

WHY DO MOSQUITOES BITE?

Mosquitoes have been around for 30 million years. During this time, they have become experts at finding people and animals on which to prey. Mosquitoes live off the blood of mammals. A mosquito is attracted to you by the warmth of your body and the chemicals that you exhale. Certain colored clothes can also make you a target.

Some mosquitoes can carry and spread diseases.

Why do bugs live on our bodies?

Not only do bugs live on your body, but they may make a home inside your body. Some bugs can crawl into your ears, dig into your skin, or feast on you while you sleep. Such creatures are parasites: organisms that live on—or in—another living being. Some parasites, such as lice and fleas, live outside your body. They are called ectoparasites. Other parasites, such as a tapeworms, live inside your body. They are known as endoparasites. Most parasites, such as lice, fleas, and bedbugs, can be an annoying problem. Don't worry. It's very rare that a bug will set up camp on—or in—you.

WHY DO DOGS GET WORMS?

There are a lot of reasons why dogs get worms, and there are a lot of worms out there. Dogs can get roundworms from eating worm eggs off the ground. Dogs can get hookworms by licking their paws after they have touched the ground where hookworms live. Some dogs get tapeworms by eating fleas that swallowed tapeworm eggs.

Ticks are not insects. They're arachnids.

HOW DO SOME TICKS SPREAD DISEASE?

Ticks are tiny animals that feed on blood. Some are as small as a sesame seed. Some ticks, such as the deer tick, can spread illnesses, such as Lyme disease, by transferring **bacteria** from animal to animal, including to humans.

Why are some animals domesticated?

Some animals, including cats, dogs, and horses, are nice to have around the house or the barn. Such animals are **domesticated**.

In other words, they have been taught to live around humans. Some scientists think that certain animals became domesticated through a series of genetic **mutations** that developed millions of years ago. Other scientists say that some animals found it easier to survive with humans around. The animals followed humans as they moved from place to place.

Why are there so many different kinds of dogs?

Why are some dogs tiny and some dogs big? Why do some dogs have lots of hair and others have very little hair? The American Kennel Club recognizes 157 dog breeds. Each breed has certain characteristics that developed over time often through careful breeding. Dogs that evolved in colder climates have thick coats to keep them warm. Dogs, such as the Chihuahua, that are native to warm climates do not have much fur, allowing heat to escape more quickly. Some dogs are more muscular than others, because they were bred to work. Some dogs are "mutts." Mutts are a mixture of many breeds. Mutts inherit characteristics from both parents.

HOW DO CATS PURR?

You've probably heard a cat purring—making a low rumbling sound as it breathes. A cat purrs when the muscles in its voice box vibrate. The muscles act as a valve for air flowing past the voice box. Cats purr when they inhale and exhale. Cats purr when they are happy or content. However, cats also purr when they are stressed out or recovering from an injury.

WHY DO LEOPARDS HAVE SPOTS?

Don't get any spot remover near a leopard. Scientists say leopards evolved with dark spots to help them hide from their prey.

Why do giraffes have long necks?

Giraffes are the tallest mammals on the planet. Some stand up to 19 feet (5.79 m) high. Some scientists think giraffes have long necks to reach leaves high on trees, especially during periods of drought. Others say giraffes have long necks to help them fight. Male giraffes use their necks as weapons, clubbing their opponents with their heavy skulls.

Why do camels have humps?

Someone might have told you long ago that the humps on camels contain water. *NOT TRUE!* The humps of camels are filled with fatty tissue. Animals, including humans, store energy in fat. When there's no food or water around, animals live off the stored fat. In the harsh dry desert, camels' fatty humps let them live for a long time without water.

Why do **birds fly south** for the winter?

Some birds—not all—pack their feathers for the winter and fly south, where it is much warmer. These birds are not only searching for a warmer climate, but are looking for food and water. The journey is known as **migration**. Before they start their trip, birds stuff themselves with food so they can store up fat that they will use as energy for their long journey.

WHY DO BIRDS HAVE FEATHERS?

All birds have feathers. In fact, birds are the only animals with feathers. Feathers keep birds warm. Feathers on wings help birds fly. Feathers on a bird's tail help it steer as it soars. Feathers also give a bird its colors. Some birds use feathers as camouflage. Some male birds—male peacocks, for example—use their feathers to attract females.

Why do **birds sing**?

Whether it's the squawk of a crow or the squeak of a cardinal, birds like to sing. Birds hit the high notes not because they are fans of rock 'n' roll, but because they are communicating with each other. Each birdcall has a different meaning. Sometimes males sing to attract a female. Other times, a male is warning other birds to keep away from his nest. Most birds only pay attention to birds that sound and look like them.

How do caterpillars turn into butterflies?

When is a caterpillar not a caterpillar? When it is a butterfly. Caterpillars turn into butterflies through a process called **metamorphosis** (met-ah-MOR-fa-sis). There are four stages of a butterfly's metamorphosis.

1. The first stage is when the adult female butterfly lays her eggs.

2. The eggs then form a larvae—the caterpillars. During this stage of metamorphosis, caterpillars have only one job—eat as much as possible. When caterpillars are fully grown, they stop eating.

3. Then they spin a cocoon. This is called the pupa stage. The pupa of a butterfly is called a chrysalis. The pupa hangs on a branch or a leaf.

4. Inside the cocoon, the caterpillar completely changes into the adult stage—a butterfly that breaks out of the cocoon and flies away.

Is it a moth or a butterfly?

Although similar, butterflies and moths have many differences.

BUTTERFLIES	MOTHS
Out during the day	Out during the night
Hold their wings above their body when they rest	Hold their wings down flat when they rest
Are very colorful	Most are not very colorful

WHY DO CICADAS BUZZ?

When summer rolls around, listen carefully. You might hear the buzz of the cicada. It sounds like an electric razor. Cicadas are insects that resemble huge flies. They buzz to attract a mate. The sound is produced by a pair of drumlike organs at the base of their abdomen. These organs vibrate at high speed, creating a sound that you hear generally between mid-July and September.

21

Why are some people taller than others?

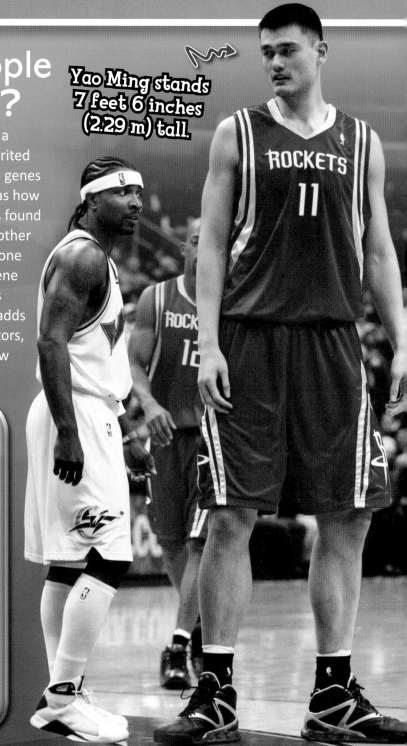

Yao Ming stands 7 feet 6 inches (2.29 m) tall.

Genes—and we're not talking blue jeans—play a leading role in people's heights. Genes are inherited characteristics such as eye and hair color. Some genes regulate our body's growth hormones, as well as how big our bones get. Moreover, in 2007, scientists found the first gene linked directly to height. As with other genes, humans inherit two copies of the gene, one from each parent. Inheriting one form of the gene adds about 0.2 of an inch (0.5 cm) to a person's height. Inheriting two forms of the same gene adds nearly 0.4 of an inch (1 cm). Environmental factors, diet, and overall health also help determine how tall a person grows.

HOW DO HUMANS AGE?

Why we age has a lot to do with hormones (the chemicals that control our body functions), our health, and our diet. Diseases later in life can affect how our brain functions, including memory and personality. Even such things as whether we're married, where we live, how much money we make, and how much education we have affect how we age.

Why do **we** cry?

Grown men cry. Babies cry. We cry when we are sad or when we are hurt. We even cry when we peel onions. Not all tears are the same, however. Sad movies or physical pain create psychic tears—tears that result from emotions. Peeling onions creates reflex tears—tears caused by irritants in the environment.

WHY DO MY EYES GET TEARS WHEN I'M NOT CRYING?

Did you know eyes squeeze out 5 to 10 ounces (150 to 300 ml) of tears a day? In fact, your eyes are full of tears right now. Every time you blink (about once every five seconds), your eyes create basal tears. Basal tears are tears that lubricate your eyeballs to keep them clean and healthy.

Why do we get **crusty stuff** in the **corners of** our eyes?

Some people call them eye boogers. Others call them eye snot. Whatever the term, it refers to the crusty stuff that gathers in the corners of our eyes, especially after sleeping. This stuff, known as rheum, is thin **mucus** that naturally seeps from both eyes, gathering and drying in the corners. Eye mucus is made up of skin, blood cells, and dust.

Why do we need food to live?

Your body needs fuel to run. That fuel comes from nutrients. Nutrients come from food. There are six classes of nutrients found in food. They include: carbohydrates, fat, protein, vitamins, minerals, and water. By giving your body the proper amounts of nutrients and energy, you're giving yourself a better chance at staying healthy.

WHY DO SOME PEOPLE CRAVE JUNK FOOD?

Some researchers say that people can become addicted to sugar and fat—the two main ingredients in junk food. One study found that a diet high in fat changes the brain's biochemistry in the same way that some drugs do. Scientists say high-fat diets release brain chemicals called opioids. Opioids reduce the feeling of being full, so people eat more. Rats in one study loved their diets of high-fat food so much that they just kept eating. The rats also loved sugar. When sugar was taken away from them, the rats' teeth started chattering and their bodies shook.

WHY IS EXERCISE IMPORTANT?

Exercise burns calories and can keep you trim and fit. Exercise also can relax you and lessen stress. Exercise keeps your body's organs, such as the heart and lungs, healthy.

You can lose 1 pound (.45 kg) by burning 3,500 calories.

Why do people go bald?

Homer Simpson used to have a full head of hair. But every time Marge told her husband that she was going to have a baby, TV's favorite cartoon dad yanked out whatever curls he had. Luckily, most people don't go bald this way. Baldness is caused by a person's genes and hormones. Genes are inherited characteristics such as eye and hair color. Hormones control how the body functions. The actual process of going bald, however, remains a mystery—except if you're Homer Simpson. Chances are if you are a guy and your dad has gone bald, you probably will too at his age!

WHY DO SOME PEOPLE HAVE MORE HAIR THAN OTHERS

Some people are just downright hairy. They have hairy arms, hairy backs, and hairy legs. Genes and hormones determine whether someone can grow a lot of hair. For some, hair grows like a weed. For others, it does not. Each hair on a person's head grows from its own hair follicle at a rate of about a half an inch (13 mm) every month.

Why does **hair turn gray?**

Hair turns gray or white because we get older. Every strand of hair has a root that keeps the hair anchored in place. The root is surrounded by a follicle under the skin. Each follicle has pigment cells that produce a chemical called **melanin**. Melanin gives hair its color. As a person gets older the pigment cells die off. As that happens, each strand of hair no longer contains as much melanin. That causes the hair to turn gray or white.

What is hay fever?

Hay fever's real name is rhinitis (rye-NEYE-tis). People who suffer from hay fever are allergic to **pollen** and other particles in the air, which affect a part of the nose. As a result, a person might have itchy, watery eyes, a stuffed nose, or a drippy throat. Dust mites, animal dander, mold spores, and fabric fibers can also cause hay fever. Nearly 15 to 20 percent of Americans suffer from hay fever. Roughly 10,000 children in the U.S. miss school each day because of hay fever.

WHY DOES POISON IVY MAKE ME ITCH?

Have you ever heard this rhyme: "*Leaves of three, let them be*"? When you're out in the yard or hiking in the woods, stay away from plants that have groups of three leaves growing together. Those plants could be poison ivy. The leaves of poison ivy, poison oak, and poison sumac produce a colorless, oil-like substance called **urushiol**. About 60 percent of people are allergic to urushiol. When they touch the leaves of these nasty plants, their skin becomes red and itchy.

Blisters often appear when someone comes in contact with urushiol.

Ah-choo!
Thousands of kids miss school each day because of hay fever!

WHY ARE SOME PEOPLE ALLERGIC TO CERTAIN FOODS?

Food allergies are very serious. Roughly 3.3 million people are allergic to peanuts. Millions more are allergic to milk, cheese, and other dairy products. Allergies develop when the body's **immune system** mistakes something usually harmless for a substance that is harmful. An allergic reaction occurs when the body tries to fight off the substance.

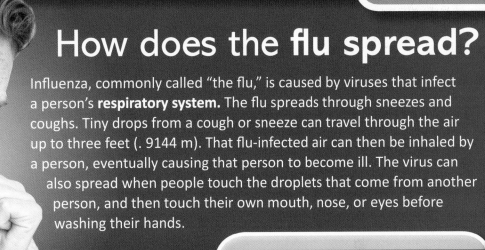

How does the flu spread?

Influenza, commonly called "the flu," is caused by viruses that infect a person's **respiratory system.** The flu spreads through sneezes and coughs. Tiny drops from a cough or sneeze can travel through the air up to three feet (. 9144 m). That flu-infected air can then be inhaled by a person, eventually causing that person to become ill. The virus can also spread when people touch the droplets that come from another person, and then touch their own mouth, nose, or eyes before washing their hands.

HOW DOES ASPIRIN CURE MY HEADACHE?

A chemical called ASA is the main ingredient in aspirin. ASA latches onto an **enzyme** in the body's cells. This enzyme creates a chemical called prostaglandin (pros-tuh-GLAN-din). Prostaglandin's job is to send messages to the brain telling it that the head is in pain. An aspirin changes the enzyme so it can no longer make prostaglandin. So, the pain messages to the brain stop, and your headache disappears. Never take an aspirin without asking for a parent's okay.

When were **antibiotics** invented?

Antibiotics are medications that kill bacteria without harming the body's cells. British scientist Sir Alexander Fleming first discovered penicillin in 1928, but it didn't gain widespread use until the 1940s, just in time to prevent infections from battlefield wounds in the final years of World War II. Penicillin has since saved millions of lives. Today, there are many types of antibiotics.

Why is **blood important** ?

Dracula isn't the only one who needs blood to survive. We all do. Blood carries nutrients to every cell in the body. Blood is a mixture of cells and plasma. Plasma is the liquid portion of blood. Red blood cells carry the oxygen your body needs to survive. Red blood cells swim in plasma, as do white blood cells, which fight infection. Plasma also carries vitamins, minerals, hormones, and other things that the body needs.

Donating blood saves lives!

Why do we bleed?

When a blood vessel is damaged, blood spews out. The bigger the hole, the more a person bleeds. As the heart beats, it pumps blood through a system of blood vessels—flexible tubes that carry blood to every part of the body. There are three main types of blood vessels: arteries, which carry blood away from the heart to all of the body's tissues; veins, which carry blood to the heart; and capillaries, which connect arteries and veins.

WHY IS BLOOD RED?

Blood contains a protein called hemoglobin. Hemoglobin carries oxygen. When hemoglobin comes in contact with oxygen, the hemoglobin changes its color, giving blood its reddish hue. You might have noticed that the veins in your body look dark. Veins look dark because the un-oxygenated blood in them is dark.

Why does the body produce saliva?

Spit is super! Spit is good! Just don't spit on the sidewalk. Spit, otherwise known as saliva, is a clear liquid that is made in your mouth 24/7. It is made up mostly of water and other chemicals. Glands on the inside of each cheek, on the bottom of the mouth, and under the jaw near the front of the mouth, produce about 2 to 4 pints (1 to 2 L) of saliva each day. Saliva makes food moist, which makes it easier to swallow. Saliva also keeps the tongue wet so you can taste foods better. Saliva helps keep your mouth clean and breaks down food before it reaches your stomach.

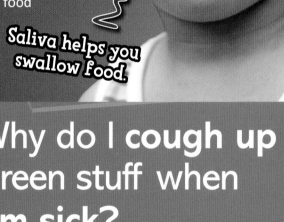

Saliva helps you swallow food.

WHY DOES PUS FORM ON A CUT?

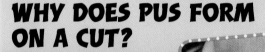

When you cut yourself, you are opening yourself up (no pun intended) to an infection. Bacteria cause infections. When the skin is punctured or cut, bacteria worm their way into the body. The body's white blood cells, which fight off infection, rush to the scene of the injury. Sometimes bacteria overwhelm the disease-fighting white blood cells. When that happens, they call for help. Pus is the result of millions of white blood cells tackling the bacteria.

Why do I cough up green stuff when I'm sick?

What you are coughing up is phlegm (flem), the sticky stuff that drips down the back of your throat when you have a cold. The respiratory system's mucus membranes produce phlegm. Viruses or bacteria will often lodge in the lungs or in some other portion of the respiratory system. When that happens, your body produces mucus to fight off the invaders. Phlegm is thicker than normal mucus. The body tries to get rid of phlegm with a cough. If phlegm cannot be expelled, it can build up and become thicker and green.

29

Why do I have a belly button?

While you were in your mother's womb waiting to be born, you had to eat and breathe. Of course, you couldn't order a pizza or go out for hamburgers, so nature gave you the next best thing—an umbilical cord. The umbilical cord connects a developing **embryo** or **fetus** to the mother's placenta, a lining that transfers blood and nutrients from the mother to the fetus. The cord's main function is to carry nourishment and oxygen from the placenta to the fetus or embryo. The cord also carries out waste material. Your belly button, or navel, is the place where your umbilical cord was attached to you before it was cut at birth.

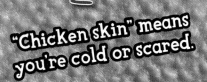

"Chicken skin" means you're cold or scared.

WHY DO WE HAVE FINGERNAILS?

You can paint them! You can bite them! You can scratch an itch with them! Fingernails are one of the things that separate **primates**, including humans, from other mammals. Basically, fingernails are flat claws. A long time ago, primates lost their claws and developed fingernails. They used their fingernails to move about and to grasp smaller objects, such as tree branches filled with fruit. When humans evolved, we kept our fingernails. They help us perform a variety of tasks, including scratching an itch, peeling a fruit, undoing a knot, and opening a package of string cheese.

Why do I get **goose bumps**?

You're watching a scary movie. Just before the zombie pokes its head out of the closet, you get goose bumps on your arms. Goose bumps, or chicken skin, are short-lived changes in your skin caused by cold or fear. Small muscles are attached to the tiny hairs in your skin. When you are cold or scared, the muscles contract, pulling the hair upright and causing goose bumps.

How can you stop the hiccups?

Sometimes people eat or drink so fast or get so excited that they begin to hiccup. Humans hiccup when something causes the diaphragm to spasm. The diaphragm is the large muscle that separates the thorax (the part of the body that contains the lungs and heart) from the abdomen (the part of the body that contains the stomach and intestines). These spasms cause you to take a breath that is suddenly stopped when the vocal cords close. The result is a hiccup. But how do you stop hiccups? There's no sure way to cure them, but you can try holding your breath for 30 seconds, then exhaling gradually. You can also breathe into a paper bag five times in a row or take several gulps of water without stopping.

Holding your breath might cure the hiccups!

WHY DO I ITCH?

A mosquito bites you. *Scratch*! *Scratch*, scratch, scratch. Itching can drive a person crazy. The skin is the largest organ a person has. It covers 20 square feet (2 sq m). Skin is exposed to things that make people itch all the time, such as bug bites, poison ivy, scratches, and cuts. Itching starts with some irritation. The itch is your body's way of telling your brain that something is wrong. People automatically scratch itches in an attempt to remove the irritant.

WHY DOES A SCAB FORM ON A CUT?

Scabs form when blood cells called platelets (PLAYT-lits) rush toward a cut when your skin is broken. As the clot hardens, it becomes a crusty and dark scab. Scabs are good. They help keep germs and other stuff out of the wound. That gives the skin a chance to heal. If you have a scab, don't pick it off. Let it fall off naturally.

31

Why do we need
to sleep ?

Yawn! It's time for bed. Sleep is important, yet scientists don't know why. Doctors recommend that most kids spend eight hours a day, or 2,920 hours a year, sleeping. Scientists believe that muscles don't need to sleep. They just need to relax every now and again. The brain seems to need to sleep, although no one knows why. One theory suggests that sleep allows the brain to review all the bits of information people gather while awake. Another theory says brains need sleep to help bodies flush out waste. Other scientists say sleep gives people the energy needed to help do things such as ride a bike or play the trumpet.

Why do we **dream?**

As is true with sleep, scientists don't really know why we dream. Some researchers say dreaming serves no real purpose. Others say dreaming is important to our mental and physical health. Some doctors say dreams may be a reflection of a person's waking thoughts and wants.

Doctors say you should sleep 2,920 hours a year!

WHY DOES YOUR BODY SOMETIMES "JERK" BEFORE YOU DRIFT OFF TO SLEEP?

You're about to drift off to sleep and your body suddenly jerks you awake. Scientists call this jerk a hypnic (HIP-nik) or myoclonic (my-uh-KLAH-nik) jerk. No one knows why this happens. Some scientists think the brain causes people to jerk because it gets confused when muscles start to relax. For a second, you think you're falling. Your brain tells your muscles to tense up to "catch" yourself before you fall.

Why don't kids who are color blind see everything in black and white?

Life isn't black and white for kids who are color blind. In fact, color blind people can see most colors. When a person looks at an object, light enters the front of the eyes through the **lenses**. Light then travels to the **retina**, which acts like a big movie screen. The retina is packed with cells made up of rods and cones. Rods help people see in black and white. Cones allow people to see objects in color. Each cone has a different **pigment**. These pigments allow a person to tell the difference between colors. Color blind kids might only be missing one particular type of cone, such as green or red. Although the person can see other colors, they might see gray for the cone they are missing.

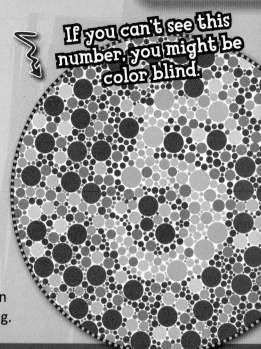

If you can't see this number, you might be color blind.

WHY DO WE BLINK?

Eyes have their own windshield washing fluid—tears. Blinking spreads tears across the eye like a windshield wiper, making sure the eyes are always clean and wet.

HOW DO EYELASHES KEEP DUST FROM GETTING INSIDE THE EYE?

Eyelashes curve up to keep water and sweat from the eye, while directing it to flow down the cheek or nose. Eyelashes also keep dust and dirt from getting into our eyes.

Why is
sweat salty?

Everyone has millions of sweat glands.

The human body is a huge saltshaker. Salt is one of the ingredients in sweat, or perspiration. When a person sweats, the body releases the watery liquid that remains after blood plasma filters out red blood cells and platelets. Plasma contains a teaspoon of salt per liter.

WHY DO WE SWEAT?

Sweating is the body's way of cooling itself off, whether a person is stressing over a big test or running around at soccer practice. Sweat comes from the 2.6 million sweat glands in the skin.

WHY DO SOME PEOPLE SWEAT MORE THAN OTHERS?

Some people who sweat a lot may have a condition called hyperhidrosis (HI-per-hi-DROH-sis). Low blood sugar and some diseases may cause excessive sweating. Medicines may also make some people sweat a lot.

Why does sweat smell?

Sweat stinks. The smell comes from bacteria that live on skin. These tiny creatures mix with sweat, causing a foul odor. So please wash up after you exercise—for the sake of all of us

Why does my nose run?

Is your nose running? Shut the door before it runs out of the house. Okay, bad joke, but many people do get runny noses. A runny nose, also known as rhinorrhea (RI-no-REE-uh), occurs when tissue and blood vessels inside the nose are swollen with too much fluid or mucus. Allergies, colds, the flu, dust, and even spicy foods can make your nose run.

WHY DOES EVERYONE GET SNOT?

Snot and boogers are just two names we give nasal mucus. Think of the nose as a vacuum cleaner, sucking in bits of dirt and dust each day. Nose hair traps that dirt and dust. Mucus surrounds the dirt, forming slimy lumps to keep it from getting into the lungs. When people blow or—*yuck*!—pick their nose, they remove all that junk.

It's not a good idea to pick your nose.

Why do I have **earwax**?

Earwax isn't used to make candles, but it does help the body defend itself against unwanted invaders. Earwax traps dirt and bacteria that would otherwise get into the ears. Too much earwax can be a problem if it hardens.

Why does my stomach growl after I eat?

Everything is quiet and suddenly—*growwwwwwwwwwwlllllll*—someone's stomach starts making a grumbling, rumbling, or sloshing noise. When Winnie the Pooh says that there's a "rumbly in my tumbly," he's trying to say the muscles in his digestive system are moving and pushing a gooey mixture of food and liquid, known as chyme (kīm), through his **digestive tract**. Moving along with the mush is air and gas, which gets squeezed, creating the noises you hear.

Why do I **pass gas**?

Everybody—from best friends to teachers—passes gas. The average person passes gas 14 times a day. Gas forms in the digestive tract and is made up of carbon dioxide, oxygen, nitrogen, and other gases. We get gas because we swallow small bits of air as we eat or drink. Gas also forms when the body does not digest certain foods. Then, the body expels gas through burping or passing it through the **rectum** as flatulence.

The smell of flatulence comes from bacteria.

WHY DOES FLATULENCE SMELL BAD?

The smell comes from bacteria in the large intestine that release small amounts of gas containing sulfur.

People with light skin often get freckles.

Why do some kids have freckles?

Freckles are batches of skin cells that contain color. Some of these cells are tan colored; others are light brown and very small. Most kids who have freckles have a light complexion. People with light, or a fair, complexion have less melanin (MEL-uh-nin) in their skin. Melanin is a chemical that protects the skin from the sun's ultraviolet rays, which cause freckles. People with fair skin are more likely to get freckles than people with darker skin.

Why do some kids have birthmarks?

Birthmarks are marks on the skin. People get birthmarks at, well, birth. There are several types of birthmarks. One, known as a **hemangioma** (hem-an-jee-OH-ma) occurs when tiny blood vessels grow in one area of the skin. A strawberry hemangioma looks like a tiny strawberry. Most strawberry hemangiomas go away. Another type of birthmark is a port wine stain, which is either purple or maroon in color.

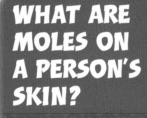

WHAT ARE MOLES ON A PERSON'S SKIN?

Moles are a collection of cells that contain color. People often refer to them as beauty marks. Moles are not painful.

What happens *when I sneeze*?

Ah-choo! A sneeze is another way for the body to get rid of **viruses**, bacteria, dust, dirt, hair, and other pollutants. A sneeze begins when the upper portion of the nasal lining is irritated by a virus or a bit of dust. Tiny nerves then send a signal, telling the brain that something isn't right. The brain orders the muscles in the chest and throat to contract, or tighten. The brain then tells the eyes to shut and the **palate** to close. *Ah-choo*! Chest and throat contractions make you sneeze. Sneezes can travel up to 100 miles (160.93 km) an hour, while sending 5,000 bacteria-filled water drops into the air.

It's impossible to sneeze with your eyes open!

Why do **people cough**?

Coughing is another way for the body to clear its respiratory system of bacteria, viruses, and other things. A cough begins when something irritates the nerves in the lungs. Mucus in the lungs traps the tiny irritants. When that happens, tiny air tubes called bronchi contract. The lungs then send a signal to the brain's cough center, telling the brain it needs to get rid of these invaders. The brain tells the glottis— two flaps of muscle that make up part of the voice box—to close. Pressure increases in the lower part of the glottis as muscles in the chest contract. The glottis reopens, and the lungs forcefully expel the air through the mouth—a cough.

Why do I feel pain when I stub my toe?

Stub a toe—*ouch*! Hit a thumb with a hammer—*ouch*, *ouch*, *ouch*! Touch a hot stove—*that hurts*! While no one likes to be in pain, pain is the body's way of telling the brain that something might be wrong. Pain travels to and from the brain along the spinal cord and nerves. Nerve cells beneath the skin sense pain. When there is an injury to the body, such as banging an elbow very hard, these tiny cells send messages to the brain, telling it that the body has been hurt.

WHY DOES A PERSON GET TIRED IN THE AFTERNOON?

A person's biological clock, known as the circadian cycle, is ticking and is responsible for afternoon sleepiness. This biological clock is affected by several things, including the release of a hormone called melatonin (mel-uh-TOE-nin). Melatonin causes sleepiness. Normally, melatonin levels rise in the mid- to late evening and remain high for most of the night. By the time a person wakes up, the level has dropped. Many people, however, get sleepy at around 3 p.m. because their bodies release a lot of melatonin at that time.

What is a **fever**?

Fevers are good. They are our body's natural way of fighting germs. A fever occurs when an army of white blood cells battles the germs. The faster the white blood cells attack, the hotter the body gets. Not everyone has a normal temperature of 98.6°F (37°C). Some are higher, and some are lower, and these variations are fine. When the body's temperature rises beyond that, it becomes a condition known as fever. There are several reasons why people get fevers. They could have an infection caused by a virus, or they could sustain an illnes or injury, such as a heart attack, heatstroke, or burn.

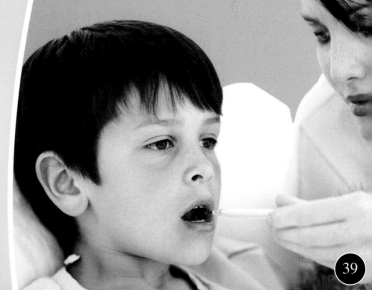

39

Why can we hear sound and see light?

Sounds are tiny vibrations, or air pressure changes, that travel as waves. These waves hit a person's eardrum. The ear then sends a signal to the brain that allows the person to hear a sound. Light is made up of tiny particles called **photons**. Photons also travel in waves, reaching the eyes, which allow people to see.

Why are som sounds loud and shrill??

We hear loud and shrill sounds because there are differences in **pitch** caused by different spaces between sound waves. The closer together the waves are, the higher the pitch. Sound waves are measured in **wavelengths**. The loudness of a sound is measured in decibels. At 130 decibels, a jackhammer makes a painful sound. A subway train whizzes by you at an extremely loud 90 decibels.

WHY DO DOGS HEAR BETTER THAN HUMANS?

Dogs can hear sounds at a much higher frequency than humans. Frequency is the number of times a sound wave vibrates in a second. Humans can only hear sounds within a narrow range of frequencies. Sometimes the frequency of a sound is so high that humans can't hear the sound, but dogs can.

Why do some older people have long ear hair?

If you are a young male, the last thing you worry about is the length of your ear hair. Like nose hair, the tiny hairs in a person's ears protect the body from dust and dirt. As a person gets older, ear hair tends to grow... and grow... and grow. No one knows why this happens. Some say a person's genes play a role in ear-hair growth. Others say hormones, or chemicals that control the activity of certain cells and organs, are the reason that some people have lots of ear hair.

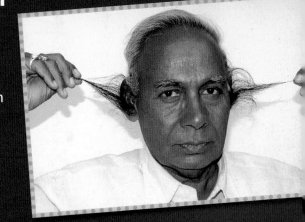

WHAT IS THE WHITE GOO THAT COMES OUT OF A POPPED PIMPLE?

The white goo is a mixture of dirt, oil, white blood cells, and bacteria. Never squeeze a pimple, because it can leave a scar.

Most warts disappear on their own.

WHY DO WARTS FORM?

A person can't get a wart from touching a frog, but a person can get a wart by becoming infected with a virus. Warts are growths on the skin caused by the human papillomavirus (PAP-uh-loh-mah-vi-rus) also known as HPV. Some warts appear on the hands and fingers. Others grow on the underside of the feet. Some warts are bumpy and rough. Others are smooth and flat. Some are yellow. Some are brown. Some are skin-colored.

41

The nose's sense of smell and the mouth's taste buds work together when people eat. The taste buds sense the taste of food (salty, bitter, sour, sweet). The nose detects specific odors. When a person chews food, the person senses the food's odor with the nose's olfactory (smell) receptors, located behind the bridge of the nose. If the nose is stuffed, the receptors won't work as well and food won't taste as good.

Why do humans have fingerprints?

The series of lines, ridges, loops, and curves on your palms and fingers are your fingerprints. Each person has a unique set of fingerprints. Genes play a part in the development of human fingerprints. However, when a baby is inside its mother's womb, it doesn't have any prints. Fingerprints develop as the baby presses against the inside of the womb. That's why identical twins have different fingerprints.

WHY DO PEOPLE GET THIRSTY?

People get thirsty because they lose more water than they drink. When your body needs water, it will let you know. Thirst receptors in the back of the throat dry up, which sends a message to the brain, telling a person to drink.

Why are people ticklish?

When someone tickles you, they are stimulating the delicate nerve endings just under the skin. Some parts of our body are more ticklish than others. Feet are especially sensitive to tickling because feet have large nerve endings.

WHY DON'T WE LAUGH WHEN WE TICKLE OURSELVES?

Try it. Not much happens, right? You might think you would feel the same sensation as if someone else was tickling you. Not so. Scientists don't know why we can't tickle ourselves. Some suspect that the element of surprise has a lot to do with it. When we tickle ourselves, we have lost the surprise. Our brain—specifically the **cerebellum**—knows what is happening and that there's no reason to laugh.

Why can we
whistle ?

People can whistle while they work, or they can whistle to call the dog. People whistle in the dark, and some whistle for fun. Whistling is a sound produced by controlling a stream of air flowing through a small hole. Most people whistle by pursing their lips together and blowing. Others can whistle through their fingers or cupped hands. People whistle to attract attention, to show approval or disapproval, or to play a song.

WHY ARE LIPS RED?

Lips are red because blood vessels known as capillaries are located near the thin skin of your lips.

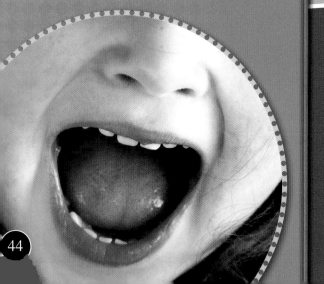

Why does it hurt to bite on aluminum foil?

Biting on foil might cause a sharp pain. That pain is a weak electric shock. When people with metal fillings in their teeth bite down on a piece of foil, the acid from the mouth's saliva turns the mouth into a battery. When teeth chomp down on foil, they receive an electric current that passes through the fillings into the sensitive part of the teeth. We don't recommend trying this!

Why do knuckles crack?

Knuckles are joints in the fingers where two separate bones meet. All of the body's joints are surrounded by a case of thick, clear liquid that keeps the **cartilage**, tissues, and muscles lubricated and nourished. Gases, such as oxygen, nitrogen, and carbon dioxide, float inside the liquid. When you bend your fingers, you stretch the case around the joint. That increases the amount of fluid. When that happens, the bubbles in the fluid begin to burst, producing a pop.

WHY DO OUR EYES TWITCH?

Eye twitching is really annoying. It can happen when you're reading a book or talking to a friend. Researchers say eye twitching is caused by muscle spasms in the eyelid. These spasms may be brought on by stress or physical eye strain.

Eyes twitch when muscles in the eyelid spasm!

Why is some hair curly?

Hair is protein. Protein contains sulfur atoms called sulfides. When two sulfur atoms come together they form a disulfide bond. The protein bends when that bonding takes place. The more disulfide bonds there are, the curlier the hair will be. People with straight hair will often curl their hair by using chemicals to create many disulfide bonds.

45

Web sites

Animals
The Animal Planet's http://animal.discovery.com/ is neat. There are games, videos, and blogs.

Earth
Take a wonderful journey across the globe with this Web site from the Smithsonian Institution: http://www.mnh.si.edu/earth/main_frames.html.

Space
NASA's Web sites are out of this world. Check out http://solarsystem.nasa.gov/planets/index.cfm and learn more about our solar system. Click on a planet and discover amazing facts.

Humans
Go to http://kidshealth.org/kid/htbw/htbw_main_page.html and learn how the human body works.

People and Places
Explore the world on http://www.nationalgeographic.com/. This amazing Web site links to parts of the world many people don't know about. You can access news features, maps, and videos and learn about many different people and places. For the latest news about people and places, go to timeforkids.com.

History
If you're a history buff, go to http://www.history.com/. Click on "This Day in History" to find out what happened on any particular day. Learn about world leaders and play dozens of games.

Science
Read more about the world of science with National Geographic at http://science.nationalgeographic.com/science/.

Technology
If you're interested in some of the dumbest inventions ever produced, the editors of Life magazine have put them all together for you at http://www.life.com/image/3270485/in-gallery/25371.

Arts and Culture
If you're interested in the art of the Renaissance, http://www.renaissanceconnection.org/home.html is a wonderful place to learn about how Renaissance artists lived and worked.

Sports
Sports and kids go together like, well, sports and kids. Keep up with all the news of sports and play some games at http://www.sikids.com/.

Book List

Animals
National Geographic Encyclopedia of Animals by Karen McGhee & George McKay, PhD (National Geographic Society, 2006)

Earth
Smithsonian Earth by James F. Luhr (Dorling Kindersley Publishing, 2007)

Space
Smithsonian Atlas of Space Exploration by Roger D. Launius & Andrew K. Johnston (Smithsonian Institution, 2009)

Humans
Human Body: An Interactive Guide to the Inner Workings of the Body (Barron's Educational Series, 2008)

People and Places
History of the World: People, Places, and Ideas by Henry Billing (Steck-Vaughn Company, 2003)

History
Children's Encyclopedia of American History by David C. King (Smithsonian Institution, 2003)

Science
The Science Book: Everything You Need to Know About the World and How It Works by Marshall Brain (National Geographic, 2008)

Technology
Computers and Technology by Tara Koellhoffer, (Editor) & Emily Sohn (Forward) (Chelsea Clubhouse, 2006)

Arts and Culture
Performing Arts (Culture Encyclopedia) by Antony Mason (Mason Crest Publishers, 2002)

Sports
The Greatest Moments in Sports by Len Berman (Sourcebooks, 2009)

abdomen the part of the body that contains the organs needed for digestion

bacteria microscopic single-celled organisms found in water, air, and soil

bioluminescent relating to animals that make their own light

camouflage a method that allows an organism to blend into its environment, avoiding detection

cartilage a flexible, rubbery tissue that cushions bones and joints

cerebellum a part of the brain that controls muscle movement and balance

circulatory system the organs and tissues that help pump blood and oxygen through the body

digestive tract the system of organs, including the stomach and intestines, responsible for breaking food down so that the body can absorb nutrients

DNA short for deoxyribonucleic acid; DNA is a spiral-shaped molecule found in the body's cells. It contains a person's genes, which determine characteristics, such as eye and hair color.

domesticated adapted to live with humans

embryo early developmental stage of an animal or plant following the fertilization of an egg cell; in humans, the term embryo describes the fertilized egg during its first seven weeks of existence.

enzyme a substance produced by cells that speeds up the chemical reactions necessary for life

evolution the theory that various plants and animals change over time to a different and usually more complex or better form

fetus a term that describes the human embryo after eight weeks of development

hemangioma a mass of blood vessels that appear as birthmarks

hypothesis an educated guess

immune system cells, proteins, and tissue that protect the body from infection and disease

lens a part of the eye that helps bring rays of light into focus

mammal a warm-blooded vertebrate (having a backbone) that has hair or fur; mammals feed milk to their young.

melanin a pigment that produces eye, skin, and hair color

metamorphosis a period during the life cycle of many insects, most amphibians, and some fish during which the individual body changes from one form to another

migration geographical movement

mucus a fluid formed in the body that lubricates and protects

mutations changes in genes produced by a change in the DNA that makes up the hereditary material of all living organisms

palate the roof of the mouth

pheromones chemicals produced by an animal that affect the behavior of other animals

photons small points of light

pigment any colors in plant or animal cells

pitch a property of sound that represents the frequency of the sound

pollen a powdery substance produced by flowers

primates animal group that includes humans, apes, monkeys, and lemurs

rectum the lower part of the large intestine

respiratory system the organs in the body responsible for breathing—the taking in of oxygen and the exhaling of carbon dioxide

retina light-sensitive tissue located at the back of the eyeball

sphenisciformes a group of birds, including penguins, that cannot fly

symbiotic the relationship between two different species of organisms that benefit one another

urushiol a toxic oil found in plants such as poison ivy

vertebrates animals with backbones

viruses tiny particles, smaller than bacteria, that can cause a variety of illnesses by entering a person's body through the nose, mouth, or breaks in the skin

wavelength the distance from the crest, or high point, of one sound, or electromagnetic wave, to the next

INDEX